STILL POINT

E MARTIN NOLAN

STILL POINT

E MARTIN NOLAN

Invisible Publishing
Halifax & Picton

Library and Archives Canada Cataloguing in Publication

Nolan, E. Martin, 1984-, author
Still point / E. Martin Nolan.

Poems.
Issued in print and electronic formats.
ISBN 978-1-926743-99-8 (softcover)—ISBN 978-1-988784-02-1 (EPUB)

I. Title.

PS3614.O467S75 2017 C811'.6 C2017-905383-3
C2017-905384-1

Edited by Jeff Latosik
Cover and interior design by Megan Fildes | Typeset in Laurentian
With thanks to type designer Rod McDonald

Printed and bound in Canada

Invisible Publishing | Halifax & Picton
www.invisiblepublishing.com

We acknowledge the support of the Canada Council for the Arts which last year invested $20.1 million in writing and publishing throughout Canada.

Canada Council for the Arts Conseil des Arts du Canada

For the people of Detroit,
New Orleans, and Toronto

Leaving the Rouge Park Inn in Dearborn,
and my friend's gone back for his phone.
So I wait alone before we part. It's quiet.
I face north towards Detroit, city of my birth.
Traffic's light. Each car is singular. The collective
chirp of the crickets is loud across the border.
They live in the column of dense woods
growing half-wild along the Rouge River.
Their invisible mass is called an orchestra
and forms a cinematic unison in the night.
I'll go that way, on the road that shadows
the Rouge through the big empty park.

A deserted shed by the road, buckling
under its roof, kneels into the tall grass.
The woods beyond it hide the river.
Across the empty plain, the other way,
a row of porch lights. People didn't flee
that block. Distant evidence of human knots
amid the vast open spaces.

I turn back to the half-wild woods. These trees
speak to each other, are wild enough for that.
They live together, holding the riverbanks in place.
The branches of the Rouge begin in the exurbs,
then merge their green silt, sliding thickly
below this canopy towards the blue Detroit.

STORM

New Orleans, 2005–2006

"Do whatchawanna!"
— The Rebirth Brass Band

Brown Pelicans return
to the Industrial Canal
after Ivan—storm that missed,
storm that turned—
to where the lake feeds the canal,
and feed on bass brought in
by the rising tide.

A woman playing hook on her porch in the summertime,
a clear drink sweating on the table beside her.

The steel and iron ring swings on its string
at a hook screwed into a square, wooden pillar.

It swings back, but bounces off her fingertips, flutters
and sways toward her face, turning just short.

Johnny Vidacovich, I watched too much TV,
and when they danced stiffly to bland music
on *Saved by the Bell* my body's natural rhythm
suffered like an under-watered sapling.
Your drum begins to help me regenerate,
with George Porter on bass, unplanned,
a lived in coherence riding on the beat.
You cast my mind elsewhere, homeward.
When I came to New Orleans, Johnny,
I wasn't lost completely. Found grace
doing figure eights on the ice when it froze
like glass in North Rosedale Park. Johnny,
we'd be there late at night, imprinting
the tight feeling of the balancing muscles
on the outside of our shins as they held us
mid-lean. First time on the ice in the winter still
lights my brain. Johnny, the plumes of breath
when we stopped—the blood fast though us
in the sudden silence was kin to
the frantic patterns you control, kin to
to the breakout of the great Red Wings
teams that made the puck a still point
as they moved it between them. Johnny,
there's a spot in the cosmic mind saved for you
and Pavel Datsyuk, a celebration of freedom
in control, time through time conquered, changed.

George grooves on something simple and you strike the side
of the kit so fast beats blur and slow—the two and four
present and kinked. Johnny, everything is fucked
and I can't carry Bush Jr.'s war dreams with me anymore.
Can't leave those dreams, though. Johnny, my brainstem
is not to understand but to inhabit. Johnny, the brainstem
is a taproot you've got to. You play a streetbeat
if it's jazz, funk, or the tippity-tappity shit tourists die for.
Once, in a duo with Mean Tim Green, you played
half the beats to an empty room at DBA
and Johnny, it's cliché, but I heard the rest.

George quotes "Joy Inside My Tears" and nothing matters
perfectly in the perfect Stevie Wonder future of now.
Johnny, I grew up where the maple keys float down
like paper jewels from the sky. Flat samaras,
is what they're called. That sounds like a tune you'd play
not trying to catch them floating down,
always of their own still point if you if you watch right.

Johnny, ice water from the ground in Harbor Springs
flows down beautiful stone canals into Lake Michigan,
past the mansions on Beach Drive, past
    perfectly pruned hedges,
past huge old willows, past sky-high property values,
to the lake turned clear-turquoise from
    the Caspian's Zebra Mussels.
Johnny, I can smell the shell-smell of the lake from here
on Oak Street by a bend in the lower Mississippi.

I remember riding in Josh's dad's old beat-up
red Firebird, the hood off-white, a replacement
from a junkyard. The muffler roared like a blast
from Skerik's electrified horn until it moved past
second gear, so the engine hummed on the freeway
and with the top down, speeding, the wind didn't whip
because the windshield made a shell of still air around us
as Weezer blasted from the speakers. We did not ask,
were we ospreys in for the kill. That moment
was every moment. Every and always and right now.

A second-line parade, back of town
on a sunny December afternoon.

Over drained swamp the band marches
past long shotgun houses.

Their horns shine unevenly, duller
where the metal rubs the body.

Nearing the steel of the I-10 overpass,
the song builds. They turn up their horns

as they arrive at the melody, and wail it
against the interstate's underbelly.

This freeway was built right through
their neighbourhood and now they make

that infrastructure sing with them, to transmit
charged melodic waves into the cars above.

The waves break through each body, though the armoured
riders cannot detect these sub-molecular effects.

For them, the city approaches or grows far.
From the freeway, you can't see where you are.

The storm Katrina enters the Gulf.

If it comes.

A system over Ohio
will pull it over us
and the hot Gulf will feed it.

It could turn.

Some ways to prepare: face the storm,
claim the wind has attained a voice.
Blow horns and beat drums against
the Mayan's one-legged god. Blow
into the coming wind and spit
flatbread made of cassava—someone
has spilled freshwater in the sea
and angered the weather-making stars.

It's ruled by chaos. It could turn.

Crouch in a communal house
around a sturdy central post.

Hurricane Katrina formed in the Atlantic
while I was in Detroit for the end of summer.
Drove down to start my final year as the storm
entered the Gulf. In Kentucky, got the call
to turn around: "everyone is leaving."

Back in Detroit, I watch the storm on TV.
Satellites show it covering the Gulf
and throwing clouds north before it,
like snow upon Louisiana. Its centre holds,
clean and strong, before the storm
turns north toward its end.

Its eye dissolves, form grows sloppy
as it spins over Ohio. The storm's rain
remains abundant over land. Katrina drenches
the heartland at the end of a dry summer.

Displaced to Detroit for the fall semester,
I half pay attention to a light course load.

Dust turns over the aisle of a city bus,
lit by the low afternoon sun.

A car stops at a red light.
No one else in sight. Runs it.

From an opening in the sidewalk
tall grasses wilt into the fall.

That November the sun never came out.
I washed dishes at Al's Rosedale Cafe,
a new soul-food place. My pants, wet,
froze on the walk home. I cut my fingers
prying at the caked ends of lasagna pans
in desperation. I lacked the tools I needed
to get things back to the way they had been.

At Al's, they slow-cooked the meat out back.
Family run, the recipes passed down
through generations from Georgia.

First thing in the morning I prepped the grill,
added hickory soaked in water and released
the rich smoke into the icy morning air.

In Mississippi, skinny pines the storm broke in half.
Then calm Lake Pontchartrain, which fed
the Industrial Canal too much water that day
when the levees failed and the waters rose.
The bridge patched with grated steel. Sections
had shifted sideways like kids' blocks in the storm.
Pelicans cruise at car-level or perch on the railing.
Like they always have. The lake calm as ever now.

New Orleans East, a suburb on the southern shore,
is mostly gone. *It looks like Detroit now*,
a friend, back earlier, said. He was right.
Like driving through the east side, down Kercheval
towards the border with Grosse Pointe. Mostly gone.

I've returned full of water-level images from TV.
Now the water's been pumped out, but a brown line
remains on each house in whole neighbourhoods,
marking where the water settled at its natural level.
And the spray-painted X on houses, marked
to say *found alive, dead animals, dead people.*

"And of the curveship lend a myth to God."
— Hart Crane

Like a bridge, a built thing, could be myth.
But what has God to do with it?
The water grows more godlike
with each year's increasing heat.
Drink from the water's moving edge.

≈

Grand Isle before sunrise. The tide comes in
and clear pools form, recede, form again.
Small birds land and feed in the moment
when the pools recede, and the wet sand
reflects like glass before refilling.

Day breaks and the tide swallows the pools.

Distant oil platforms' tiny fires
join the sky's temporary orange.

I walk down a point reaching south into the Gulf.
A curve reveals a platform, dwarfing me.
Its massive girders are too close. It
should be far and unknowable.

≋

The Gulf proceeds northward,
shoulder to the wetlands.

What we could've not done
is our shot at the miraculous.
If we can undo what we've done,
we don't know. Don't count on it.
To be saved from our engineering
by more engineering—this time
from the best part of us, we swear.

≋

Uptown at the levee, lights of the refinery
across the Riverbend at night.

Winter trees on the banks don't hide the flames
burning off excess gas. Against the dark smokestacks,

those orange points are just so many candles.
Stand just so, my dear. They become your stunning jewelry.

Cat at the foot of the driveway,
tense, ready, and right to be.
After all, you don't know me.

The house is on cinderblocks
and you run under it
to the litter you hide there.

I've just picked out cereal
after selecting a sympathy card
for a friend whose twin, on a third tour,
has died in Iraq. As far as you know,
cat, I'm human. I'll skin your young
as quickly as I'll care. You can't know
that I choose life, Cinnamon Life.

"I listened to hymns and asked so much
of them they quited
like a body that withers when if feels itself
clung to."
— Katie Ford

Mardi Gras and I can be
forgetful. A flood relieved a lake
of a terrible burden. After,
a car adrift in the upper branches
of a live oak explained nothing.

Jackson Avenue, Mardi Gras morning.
An Indian tribe heads into central city
carrying a shit stereo. No drums,
half-constructed suits, and missing
members. But the tradition continues.

Cops maintain the parade's border, but looser
than ever. Drunks cross the street easily,
high-fiving, even, as they do.

Zulus from South Africa, here
in support of the Krewe of Zulu,
turn off Jackson onto St. Charles.

It's like I dream this parade, but awaken
at Mayor Ray Nagin, who somehow
never planned for a flood, who failed
his people, like the governor and the president
failed their people. Nagin was on horseback
and in military dress, a tribute
to General Honoré, who ordered guns down
in the storm's wake, when they were
aimed at citizens in the streets.

≋

Maybe this followed Nagin in a wave down St. Charles:
not memory, but the present re-awoken for an instant.
But then I snuck past. Nagin ceased. The storm halted.

The sky was turquoise air made of sky
and brimming with melody. I was a tall blade of grass
drinking beer in the sun, then going downtown.

This is not survivor's guilt. I was always gonna leave.
To leave is a privilege that I have, just as it was
to come here to study and be a drunken fool
who was never given any trouble.

The city is there, wounded and there,
and I am moving north for more school.

A window propped open
by an empty bottle of rum.
A wind blows the curtain in, revealing

an easy shadow on the near roof
and evening sun on the tall maples beyond.

The window's skirt, begging me—
this shade, that soft evening bark.

FLIGHT

Detroit, 2007

"Let vanished rooms, let dead streets tell."
— Robert Hayden

In Detroit for the summer and I've got time.
I want to see the city I drive through,
so I reject the efficiency of the freeway,
take Grand River from downtown
to North Rosedale Park. A straight path
northwest. Forty-five minutes. No traffic. Just out
of downtown, a mansion, French revival
from 1900. Framed by a sturdy iron fence,
each bar topped by points like spear tips.

My car's alone as the red light turns green
at West Grand Boulevard. Beyond that,
the street lights go dark. The city can't pay.
Bankruptcy is inevitable, illumination sporadic.

I-96 is a block away and parallel to Grand River
as I pass the Grand Ballroom, a late sixties rock mecca,
shuttered since '72. It opened to host big bands,
was renowned for its hardwood dance floor, now rotting,
turning to humus, wanting a forest from itself right there.
Trees grow now from gaps in its red tile roof.

The intersections are brightest where, twice, the freeway crosses below. There the gas stations shine against the shine of the fast food joints—birds of the oasis.

Past the two dead hands of the giant clock
on the empty Mammoth Shopping Center,
real estate values rise and the street lights are on.

After the bright billboards above the Southfield Freeway, I turn right onto Bretton Drive, Rosedale's sporadically-lit central roadway. Big brick colonials keep a steady watch, accruing value in a rising market, as the city nears bottom.

An empty building with a ripped poster
from a failed campaign nearly two years back
on the window's plywood patch.

The building's corners were styled
and some of that tile lasts: remains of blue,
once casually admired in passing, bits of dull red,
the semblance of a symbol. A surplus hour was spent
to lay that. This was a bank, maybe a law office.

Someone approaches on foot. Looks back
from the doorless doorway. Enters.

A few cars pass—
loner herd animals.

The freeways built the metro area that would need them.
In Oakland County, Southfield Road dips below Eight Mile,
becomes a freeway entrenched through Detroit.
It emerges in Dearborn with exits to Henry Ford's invention
of history: a village of moved or replicated landmarks,
a grand estate, Ford Motors HQ, Fairlane Mall.
View of Grand River from the Southfield: a green exit sign.
View of Detroit: roofs and healthy, green tree crowns.
Take the Southfield to I-96. Downtown in twenty.

Money here, it moves. The passageways are greased.
The Lodge Freeway was the first built below ground.
Just north of Eight Mile, there's an exit to Northland,
the nation's first mall. The mall-freeway was built
symbiotically. Acres of parking lot surround the anchor,
a Hudson's when Hudson's existed, then a Macy's
and finally, an empty Macy's. Seen from the sky,
it's an empty thought bubble growing off the freeway.
Old photos show the lots bursting with American cars
shining in the sun. You can drive across its empty lots now.

The Mammoth Shopping Center was
a Federal's, then Ed's, then Mammoth.
The customers moved up to Northland.
The clock on Mammoth's central tower never moved
in my memory. It was always just past twelve thirty.

The demographics of Redford are changing.
Telegraph Road is the mighty western border
of Detroit. Eight lanes of fast heavy traffic
cut through by a broad grass island. One day
during a high-school summer I worked
in Redford planting bushes at a judge's home.
As we were wrapping up,
he stared off to the middle distance
of the golf course across the road
and predicted Blacks would move in.
I kept quiet on that. It was a dirt road.
I could not read his fear. The demographics
of Redford did change. Blacks started moved in.

This city was collided together. The suburbs
are where a lot of it bounced to.

People generally get off of leaking ships
and trees drop their leaves when they're sick.

The Jefferson North Assembly Plant stretches
from Jefferson north to Mack, cutting blocks
adjacent to it off from Detroit. The border cuts
them off from Grosse Pointe. A square mile
boxed in. Rich grasslands, scattered houses,
full trees turns to Norman Rockwell across
Alter Road—line on a map as portal.

If you cross Alter Road, pick the right spot.
Cross from Detroit to Grosse Pointe not
on the main routes. The contrast is muted.
Take Vernor, through the middle of it.

Check Google maps, on satellite view.
The grass isn't always greener across the road
but on the Detroit side there's way more of it.

"Divorce is
the sign of knowledge in our time,
divorce! divorce!"
— William Carlos Williams

Let's think of the city strictly as a tax base.
Think of divorce—divorce!—as its logic.
As such, it has had one, but all along
the city was internally—divorced!—
a tax base always apart from itself.

The less a base there is
the less there can be one.
Logic of the melting iceberg.
Logic of a metropolitan area
turned against its centre.

People did things but people didn't do this
whole thing. A people did not do this.
The things we do touch the things we do,
then bloom in the beautiful global economy.

What brought people here went somewhere else
and it can and has left there too. Northland Mall
is closing. Youngstown, downsizing. Money here,
it moves. You cannot bet your home on a roamer
unless you can roam with it, so roam wildly
new world stumbler. Yours you will have
never planned.

Two ashes stood out front the house for years,
dead. The lone elm thrived. Elms once vaulted high
over the family homes of Detroit, "the city of trees."
Dutch elm disease wiped them out. This one lived,
was immune, a cousin species to the fallen canopy
and planted after their bodies were shipped away.

Ashes were planted all over to replace the elms.
Then the emerald ash borer came. Without predators,
it gorged below the bark on the flow from the roots
to the crown. It has wiped out most of the ashes.
The huge ash out back got cut down first.
It was on our land, and likely to rot and fall.
Below the bark, the softwood was covered
in hundreds of crisscrossing paths. A cut throat.

The husks out front were on city land. The city,
in debt and broke, was slow to remove them.
The bug came on crates from Asia and did
what it did. The emerald ash borer won.
It was a huge American success story.

Suckers shot from the roots of the dying trees.
They grew with surprising vigour. Large, dark leaves.
Each sucker was a clone of its dying mother plant.
A futile attempt to revive, for the bug comes back.

Ash can be a forest or frontier tree. A stump in the forest
can live on the roots of its family. These were alone
in an unnatural frontier, and their death was fast.

I was told to cut down the suckers. Tough and bendable,
they didn't cut cleanly. The green wood bled on my hands.
I couldn't cut the suckers close to their base. The stems
looked at me, sugar-water dripping from their open bark.

Man at a red light on the service drive
beside me, you're in the lane that merges.
Your phone shines on your expressionless face.

You will jump on the freeway, head north
out of the city. Your engine heat's just for you
and for who you go home to.

But if we broke our margins, if I swerved
when the light says go, bumped you,
cracked a harmless tail light—
our doors would need unsealing.
Bodily on the roadway, we'd pass
insurance papers between us in the night.

My friend in the car beside me,
we would have no barrier between us.
We would know the sound of our voices.
We would exchange phone numbers.
We would hold each other responsible.

We don't. I hear your engine cue up, barely.
You join the freeway and I turn off
the service drive, headed home.

You refused to leave, an outlaw
hunting squirrels, Muley Graves,
you did not own.

Tom Joad fought hard, spoke out
for the poor, Muley Graves,
he blessed the weak.

His fame's been sung by Bruce and Rage,
he's a hero, Muley Graves,
but how 'bout you?

No one ever made a song, or sung,
for the ghost of Muley Graves,
who stayed, who lost.

I can't produce the voice or face,
make a me out of Muley Graves,
far-off, worn.

I don't have dust in my white face.
I want to forget you, Muley Graves,
and shit, I will.

I cannot know the way you know,
I can't be you, Muley Graves,
from what I know.

I've worked, been a system's latch,
Muley Graves, I've owned little
but not like you.

I've owned a life of comfort
and head starts, Muley Graves,
and gotten by.

You were more white than the natives
you displaced, Muley Graves,
but less than me.

You felt you were native to the land,
Muley Graves, and likewise
were told "now leave."

I left my home by choice,
Muley Graves, and loved
the place I went to.

That place was nearly all drowned
Muley Graves, while I looked
down from high ground.

The world's a shitty guitar
unless it's re-strung, Muley Graves,
and we haven't always tried.

I can't sing, though I've sung,
for your ghost, Muley Graves,
or, Lord, I've tried.

The Grand River exit of the Southfield Freeway.
By the autoshop, a Wendy's,
a Rally's by the carwash, get fried fish
at the old White Castle. All cars
and cars buying food.

                                        Never since
have I wanted like I once wanted the wet flavour
of that billboard-predicted mouth orgy.

And you know fucking what? It was like that.
I reaped openly every bit of its teenage-applied,

probably spit-on, maybe even—I shouldn't
go there. But damn—did it seem to me
that meat, that cheese, such chemical mask,
to rise even above the greatness
promised by the billboards towering over the off ramp
like bare willows by a dry riverbed, far taller
than any business tower or steeple in sight. Lit all night.

The way the car turns left off the service drive
is written into the instinctive movement
of the middle part of my body. This
will always be home.

BOOM

Toronto, 2008

"Markets no longer appear in the entirely rational, well-behaved patterns of past financial theorists."

— Benoit Mandelbrot

In the light over the back alley, a heavy-blowing snowfall
swirls into that big public light, and is as easily taken away.
I read that the beauty of illusions makes them real
in an essay called "Beautiful Snowflakes." That light goes out,
as it does. But out the small window above the sink,
facing the neighbours, my small lamp shines.
I glimpse snowflakes blown between the row houses.

I turn out my lamp, a lighthouse not altering the snow's course.
The window is a blur, reflecting a lamp across the room.
I hear the wind turn through the brick, carrying crystals.
My reflection covers the window.
Some things aren't known. I flick the lamp back on,
inflict the dark with reports of its snowflakes.

I've seen more sunsets looking east
than I have looking west.

Both horizons are blocked from me
in my second-floor apartment.

Eastward, glass towers reflect
just one shade of western sky.

I cannot go to bridges over train tracks
to watch the sunset true. It's cold.

The oranges cut with purples,
lemon yellow, all on a rich pink base,

made more beautiful by the smog,
more red, the colour of love—

looking east, each window's a pixel
like an orange sequin.

In the rooms behind that sparkle
someone normally watches sunsets.

The grey piles of mining waste
out the Greyhound's right window
look like snow-covered mountains
when seen in the left window's reflection.

Late winter and the snowbanks
are ash-grey. They reveal
tossed cigarette butts.
Cherries tunneled into snow mounds
that were bright for a day.

Early morning, the red-tail's on the pear tree's
bare knuckles, scaring the shit out of the squirrels.

The hawk isn't about them. It doesn't even flinch
when I open the creaking door, step out to the porch.

We are at eye level and it faces me with a dead, unflinching
stare. Sees through me, silently unimpressed.

The sun is orange-veiled and smudged above the hospital
and I am making myself late, missing breakfast, watching

the hawk. It leaps to the lamppost above the alleyway
then takes off, soars above the yards, watching the ground.

Minutes later she flies low over the alley, hunting. Swerves
into a backyard and below view. A raptor is never late.

"Please move back to make room for other passengers."
— Toronto Transit Commission

A packed streetcar's a collective
half-acknowledgement of strangers.
I wedge into the crowd. Two doctors,
dapper, squeezed behind me, barely
in the door, calmly talk databases.
An old woman grips the support bar
firmly, covered head tucked low.
The cracks in her knuckles are close
enough to see the chalky white of them.
My arm's over her as I grab the bar
that four others hold. One is drunk.
I face backward, nothing to lean on.
The drunk woman faces me, smiling,
talks friendly to a man facing her.
I can see only parts of the bodies
of the other riders, though I bump them.

Someone bends down and I catch
in a middle window the reflection
of a man near the back. He has room.
His feet are spread for better balance.
They don't know to make room for us,
to move back. To care. They don't listen.
This man doesn't even know about us.
Someone unbends and the scene is gone.

In our front cluster the drunk woman
fondles the man she speaks to, who shifts
unwillingly, bumping someone else. She points
odd arrangements of fingers at him,
stopping on something like a hook,
then slowly lowers her hand.
Her laughter is hot vodka air.
Her other hand slips from the bar
and touches the other hands.
The roomy back is an ocean away.
They have choice in positioning their bodies.

One of the doctors says, *skip the online system,*
it's shit, call—then the floating ground we share
leans hard on the brakes just as the streetcar
turns into Bathurst Station. The horn
blares. My grip breaks free and my hand
touches three other hands.

I hold, to my side, the old woman tilting
below me as I sway, the back of my free hand
brushing another hand, a face. The streetcar stops.
The driver shouts. But nothing lies dead
on the tracks. Inside we are whole, intact.
So we move forward, restore balance,
untouch, erase past eye contact. Doors
open to the world, where we all move freely.

East side of the Don Valley as night sets in.
I nod, and sometimes they don't, but it's men,

men with dogs like any man ever with any dog
on nights like nights were and still are, home

from the downtown core. The towers of Bay Street
above the horizon—but what are they hunting?

Headlights flow from the core—
a vertical, binging synapse above all

but the sky's darkening it blocks:
the city turning on, a rival moon.

The fog lays down
on Bay Street's towers,
lit by the city turning on.
We watch, smoking,
from a fifteenth-floor balcony.

It's mostly paper now, toss it,
he says, knuckles wave

it away. But it will need
direction. *Give it*
agency, he says. Flicked
at the thousand floors
of conglomerates,
boardrooms where
maybe someone looks back,
where the market metaphysics
(access restricted) are formed.

The gesture doesn't carry
the scorn I meant. The paper's taken
by the wind, sent southward
toward the lake. It lives
briefly on the air, in grace.

Unwitting olive branch to Bay Street,
steel in a glass fog, in fog.

A crane grows from the cavity dug
into the ground's gums, where the roots
of a condo are being planted.

The foundation takes years.
Then the floors emerge as a plane.
The spaces between fill in with uniform
condo walls—a blue-green glass rash
spreading across the core.

Jagged concrete boulders line the shore
outside Ontario Place, sunk into the blue-green
jelly of the lake's floor. The concrete holds in the infill
the lakeshore is built on, a cover-up people roam.
Carcasses of livestock, broken boats, the garbage
dumped in the former lake shallows, rest below.

From that built shore, in an empty parking lot,
the calm harbour waters reflect
the towers of the downtown core, and music bounces
distantly from the lakefront amphitheater,
fading in and out on the wind's whim.

Goldfish thrive in these waters. They grow
into their context, as big as dinner plates,
rampage the shoreline. Flushed down the toilet,
a funeral shameful for its lack of sacred vibes
and because the damn fish wasn't dead.

Two swans approach. One lifts it legs and ass up,
neck stretched down, mouth working
the concrete. The slime layer, brown blubber
on top of the still water, jiggles at the effort.

The swan rises, chewing algae,
recoils its neck,
the top curve of its neck
evenly, softly rusted yellow.

A french fry basket bobs upright, a napkin unballing
atop a ketchup flood.

A plastic bag floats in from the harbour,
snagged on a rod sticking out of the concrete.

September 29, 2008, day of wonder,
of the great stock market crash.

A view of the core's bank towers from a roof
in Kensington Market. The burgundy of ScotiaBank,
TD with two (one black, one tan),
Trump Tower Toronto still a hole
in the ground—the tallest of them all, the tower
of the Bank of Montreal!

It's fall, so the wind is trying
the leaves' bonds. All the bankers
have one ill-equipped follicle
with which to keep the core warm.
It tries, manic, unasked for.

The market apparatus, peaked
by faith in its faith in itself,
pulls itself, not knowing
the way forward, apart.

A pilgrimage to the core
in pursuit of sources—

the bagpiper's below the stock ticker
at the base of the tallest tower of them all.

The pillars have gone white in lifting
all the pins of all the accounts held
by the Bank of Montreal. White stone
citadel of the core, rock on which we trust!

The pit that precedes the condo
is below me. The plywood tunnel
holds me. Its outsides depict
a beautiful life in the condo to come.
Whitman would be like, *I love you*
already in the sky that will be built into.
The ads on the plywood don't say that.
They say you'd be hip if you lived here.

Through the wire fence, my back
to the unpainted inner-splinters,
the pit is collecting puddles
around the roots of its beams,
which stand like unfolded staples
punched from within the earth.

By the wrist, you take my hand
off the fence, this airy lining.
You turn me to you, draws nails
across my palm, wake of them
through this pit's mark on me, residue
granular, stirred like digital dust.

SPILL

New Orleans, 2010

"How do you represent a place where there is no edge?"
— Jeff Carney, director of Louisiana State University's Coastal Sustainability Studio

The oil well will gush for weeks,
if not forever. Unable to rest its leak,
it can only spread. Let us weep
for its incapacity, beat our dashboards
for its inability to halt
as we do, loving in spurts.
But why harness, why aim love,
a limitless capacity, more,
break the meter, rip up notations,
play what you fucking feel, let it leak,
fill the gulf between what's what and what's coming.

Oil tankers are riverboats without brass bands,
their drums filled with rhythmless crude.
How we got back, Rick's new car, three-thirty AM.
His last had no brakes, and he's now without brakes,
yelling at strangers out the window:
do you have a good heart?

He is doubting the goodness of most hearts,
but he does not doubt the heart of Jules, who is sober now,
who is good, whole, thriving, in town like me,
but avoiding Rick and this moment, this ride, and Rick
forgives him.

But shame is a square of styrofoam dragging past
three women outside the Royal Street Bar.
Rick questions: *have you a good heart?* They decline to say,
but declare they have good livers,
hoisting their beers at four AM.

Rick hiss-laughs as we jerk away
from a man standing in the street, glaring down
into Rick in response to the question.

We failed to determine the goodness of that man's heart.

Forgive me. On the freeway, Rick dares you to fear, Catriona,
and the untouchable lights of that American interstate
touch you in a bright and fearful rhythm.

It was good before, on Frenchman Street.
An old friend who asked if the bass drum lost
its CAPLOCKS when I moved to Canada—he played,
    killed it.

He promised the next day to play again with Jules,
the first time in years. They'd been close once.

Another driver took us down for a swamp tour.
This was days after the rig blew up in the Gulf.
Hard to tell a bayou from a canal down there,
one the finger of god, the other a shipping lane.
Our guide, a retired fisherman, explained a small flame.
They'd reopened the valve to release the natural gas
that props up the wetlands after the price of gas shot up.
Such methane fields are called biogas, same as landfills.
Hardly mentioned the spill, called the gators over
    in Cajun French,
fed them marshmallows, like normal. Showed us a
    cypress forest
clear-cut to the horizon. The state hardly even got
    money from it.

The well is gushing if I feast that night or not. I do.
We get po' boys and split a gumbo with gator sausage
at the Parkview Diner. Shit is delicious. The beer is $2.50,
and at sundown we walk Bayou St. John. A family
kayaks there, joyful on the calm, still waters.

The gators are forgiven for eating their young. Pregnant
each year, up to seventy times, addicted to the burden.
        The storm
is forgiven. Way to the swamp, the driver held the mirror
long fallen from the windshield—the glue still showed—
to see how his jokes went over, and to check traffic.
"Hey, Doctor!" he addressed an old, sleeping German,
a mumbling refugee of Bourbon Street, who must be forgiven.

The driver began with the bold and smiling claim
that he knew every language on Earth and he proved this
by saying *hi* in three of them, including English.
We did not return his inspired belly laughs;
we laughed to ourselves, mildly ashamed and thankful.
He beat his dashboard anyway and its ends bent up,
accustomed to the pounding of a man's fist.

Rick got us home that first early morning. We finished
the whisky then.

Two trees in front the house
held starlings that screamed from dusk to dawn
for two weeks each year.

The birds made a mad sound like the noise
of sidewalks being sawed apart.

Rick suspected their fierceness was personal,
of the unwittnessable sparks within tightening brakes,
a prophecy of the accident we should've had.

We are not condemned for the many recognitions
of the weaknesses of others, the only
kind thing

sometimes. Forgive us.

The oyster shell's in its flesh.
Just south of the party
a dark freedom uncurled
one trillion fists,

the oyster shell's in its flesh.

Stretching, the fists,
by nature not lured,
all angles at once,

the oyster shell's in its flesh.

A new method, the "top hat,"
has failed to plug the well.
Tarballs on Dauphin Island. Cars
stalled all over. Mid-Southern states
jacking gas prices up. The rig
latched to the Gulf bottom,
an invasive shellfish,
brought so low
that caps on the top hat
freeze and clog. The oil
can't come up right,
can't keep it down.
Tanker's there
if there's anything to refine.

We didn't pay to get into Fort Morgan, before Katrina,
before his breakdown, when we visited his family.
The sunset built a gradient from maroon to lemon.
We walked on the wall of the old fort's perimeter.
It lined the beach, and never faced the Yankee invasion
from the sea it was built for. Unless I was that invasion.

Rigs out to the horizon, affixed to the horizon,
far enough to merge into one distance.
The sky wore them like earrings.

That was years ago. Jules is home now, cobbled back together
like we begin. I haven't told him what I saw back then,
that it wasn't a lessening, but a recognition,
the worst, that beauty can be too pure, that its reserves
can overtake our technology. Jules, what I saw
was not madness, not at all. It was power,
and you will always have that, whether you're back home,
switching to bass, or if you're roaming the streets
wrapped in a blanket, shouting a dear friend's name,
and having that dear friend come save you. With us,
the walls of Fort Morgan have no chance against you.

BP has inserted a tube
into the runaway well
to carry off some crude,
to be refined, while the rest spills.

Inside the loosening universe
is our—
Inside the tipped galaxy
is our—
Inside the aftermath of solar creation
is our—
Inside the sky's gas ocean
is our—
Inside the Gulf's gouged floor
is our—
Inside the gathering oil plume
is Jazz Fest.

❧

At the brass-band stage of Jazz Fest,
after a short rain, a mother thinks back
to how, as a girl, she loved the moment
when the puddles settled. She looks
to her young son, in rain boots splashing
to the music in a strange rhythm
only his brainstem can compute.

Half the band's houses took eight feet
of water mixed with crude in the flood.

What I want is to cry
as the mother would cry, with focus,
in that moment, just one tear,
for what's stacked on her,
her son, filling by the gallon.
The bottom of life
is the end and his, she fears, is top-heavy
in its ease. It won't hold anything,
is in fact more pipe than cup,
a section of pipe, of pipeline,
a thing to be passed through.

I want that tear like glue. Right.

The oyster shell's in its flesh.

We lure with weakness
and weakened we need
all the dead deep murals.

The oyster shell's in its flesh.

Deep need makes moral
what cash takes like it's cash,
but the while will pursue it.

The oyster shell's in its flesh.

The oyster bed's a fragile
flesh. Oil waits for a storm
to surge it into the oyster bed.

The oyster shell's in its flesh.

I know, not just here,
the order is flipped,
first I, then the world.

The oyster shell's in its flesh.

Reports are the escaped crude
has formed a great plume
below the surface of the Gulf.

Not one ounce of the pesticides in me
wants to enter the plume,

but I must. I will offer myself to BP.
I am the humble servant of oligarchs
and their bystanding shareholders.
I will honour the innocence of the 401K,
its utter dependence.

Now take me to your submarine
with the diamond cutting blades
and HD cameras. I will ride its back
because it is a whale, and the mother of us all.

I will be armed with each brackish bead of sweat
resting on Shannon Powell's bass drum.
I will lace each tear dropped for the drowned
with Corexit and give to the plume our grief.

For using Corexit, Nalco Company will sue me,
claiming copyright infringement, and in settling
I will offer so much more than they ask for,
what they could never have—my mortality—
and I'll take unto me the horrible eternity
of the never-born corporate self.

"Top kill," the latest method, has failed to plug the well.
The moon is too strong. It cannot have the Gulf,
but pulls on it, each day, moving the tides,
flushing life through the delta, the city's canals,
where it is waited for, by pelicans and humans
alike, both singing for the accidental benefits
the moon's jealousy brings. The tides throw off
efforts to stop the gush, spreading the oil, freeing it.

The moon dreams most of oil, remembers
the life it was, has not forgotten
oil's ancient, unjust burial—and now
we've given the moon its chance.
The moon resists us. It pulls on its lover.
It can only pull, and it will forever.

Seen from the spill's live cam, the oil
is a dark jet, like a bull market.
We can watch it all day long.

Later, we'd learn that BP filmed it in HD,
but we got a heavily pixilated stream on nola.com.

Real time is to be shared. Clarity is different.

The relief wells are near completion.
The spill has been plugged for good.

The oil plume's togetherness is in dispute,
like a god at the onset of an enlightenment
that fails to disprove divinity.

Some reports claim the plume is intact, the size
of a small Caribbean island. Others claim
it's dispersed across the Gulf in single droplets,
broken off and coated in Corexit, the soap
that slides it off its whole, as we are slid
off the hinge that turns us together.

To go out as one did, when he went missing,
to search the streets, gather Jules back in,
a hand around his bare shoulder.
To sit with Rick and his questions—
to sit with anyone. To forgive
failures and know the people
you forgive once, barely,
will need forgiveness again
and might not deserve it.

One theory claims the Corexit-coated droplets
remain in a plume, drawn to each other
despite the chemicals meant to divide them.
This theory holds that the droplets transcend
the lubrication that coats them: they are deceived,
kept from touching, but joined anyway.

Friend, we depend on a hinge together. We can
take it apart, we can let it break. We can
maybe see it if it might last. We can be
the still point of the turning hinge.

It doesn't matter what Skerik played as a "routine buck"
was reported from the well. It was more. Pressure
mounted on the Gulf's floor.

When, on the surface, an English-prof-turned-rig-hand
worried fluids were used
not because they were right, but because BP had them in
surplus, it didn't matter.

No one listens to the humanities anymore. It doesn't
matter if the executives
onboard got bonuses for cost-cutting and sped-up schedules.

It might matter what Randy Ezell said to his wife
before he was called back, because the tapped gods
had grown restless.

The spill was reported a week before Jazz Fest.
I was working in a basement
prep room, plugging my own well, one fucking peeled
onion at a time.

That doesn't matter. Jules was in Alabama, saying over Skype
that James Jameson could contain such energy, keep it firm
in the pocket.

Skerik moved to New Orleans shortly after myself. After
a show, Jules would shake
his head and laugh that peculiar Alabama laugh, say,
that guy is—what.

It doesn't matter if Skerik planned what he played
as the spill began,
or where, if it went from Dizzy
to Cobain to Duke,

or if he just did a straight-up version of "Moanin'"
with a rap beat.
It does not matter because the rig was not a meditation
upon the well.

Music is a meditation upon time and sound. The well
is not until the rig makes it so.
Music has its own will. It precedes containment. To tap
the well was our choice, our will.

One Jazz Fest, me and Jules were broke as hell. I could get
a six-pack,
he had some 'shrooms left. Herlin Riley played
like a god's will at Donna's.

It was hot, so the door was open. We listened
from the street corner.
Ecstatic friends, music students, visited us on
smoke breaks. They taught me

what syncopation was, what the pocket was, how sturdily
Herlin owned it.
The music taught me it was a hell of a thing to meditate
upon it thus.

The well is declared dead.
The plume is in dispute.
The seafloor is in dispute.
BP will pay the bill. Or someone will.

The cost will be in dispute.
The shell is in the flesh.
Shrimp eat the seafloor.
I am the seafloor, burst open.

Life is the choice to eat yourself.
That might be done carefully.
The Gulf had delicious shrimp.
If it will again is in dispute.

The shell is in the pearl. The Gulf's
oxygen levels are in dispute.
The well is declared dead. If whales
can dodge the plume is in dispute.

The Gulf's known pods are undetected.
The reservoir below the well remains bountiful.
In a thinner and thinner wind, our mind.
BP will have to find the money somewhere.

Nalco's stock. Haliburton's stock. BP still exists.
The shell is in the flesh, with our mind.
Maybe good or nothing—nothing.
Still a thinner and thinner wind.

And our fate's faster in it.
The while will keep up.
The while will pursue it.
The seafloor is not a betting man.

If the while is in dispute.
Thinner, thinner.
Maybe computers.
Maybe they transcend, become the Earth.
The oyster shell's in its flesh. Cover it.

After Emily Dickinson's "Because I could not stop for Death" and the Coca-Cola Ad "It's the Real Thing."

"If I could buy the world a Coke"–
ghost Emily of Jingles
don't. It could be not quick —
the rest of slow shingles.

Buy the world nothing more.
Or, a Coke laced
with arsenic—for us dumb
and blinded—an escape.

The Earth doesn't need us,
the mountains we cast
of Waste—vulture encircled
landfills driven past.

We trust the bridge will hold—
the bridge will not break—
what hope—love held still—
what lust from Death to take.

Ghost Emily, end us full—
from your depth, rise—
we stop for only you.
The Earth, Emily, will thrive.

THE PEACE NORTH AMERICANA

every and always and right now

"I wish I had a river to skate away on."
— Joni Mitchell

On most Mondays I recover an inability
to watch. But now, in an open office hour,
I watch the ledge outside the window.
It's concrete, worn by forty years
of the wind whipping to or from
Lake Ontario. The ledge has a topography.
It's a desert sand ocean in slow motion.

Blown and bouncing off the window
and landing in a divot on the ledge,
a two-winged thing, holding seed.

From an ash, maple? How detached?
Loosened by a common sparrow?
I cannot tell you. Is this too late?
It's fall, and getting cold. I don't know.

Will the bud be taken, spread and grow?
Will it stay on the ledge, freeze, then split?
Fall, and break? Are these scraggly birds,
not native to this place, even capable—
living on our landscaping and garbage—
of aiding the spread of trees? Where here
would a tree grow naturally? I don't know.
I can't even see it if I step back, into the room.

Invested much in the individual soul. Bet the world
on it. All we were ever going to do. What a show, though.
The bright lights at the end of the world.
The bright lights of the screen remake the day.
Walked the Leslie Street Spit today. First thing I saw
when I reached open lake was a great egret,
low over the water, tracing the shore, neck folded for flight.
This peninsula is a dump for waste from large-scale projects.
And a bird sanctuary. Sometimes we try, we really do.

A patch of cottonwoods where dozens of grey birds
stand sentry over their high nests. I identify them later
through the screen's light. Black-crowned night herons.
Not an unstressed syllable until the hollow end.
How the world ends, a deep bass drum on each count,
then a skipped beat sounding everything we've ever heard.

Afternoon of the hottest July day on record.
The squirrel slides along the porch railing,
eyes the low blue tub I've filled
with suspect dirt and a tiny handful
of wildflower seeds I never watered.

The squirrel is in the low corner of the tub,
where nothing, not even a weed, has grown.
The squirrel rolls in this rare spa, rubbing its hands,
then settling in to do some scratching in repose.
Then it sees me, or thinks so. It's stock still. Me, too.

The tiny brain that relieves the squirrel of all
but the necessary past forgets me
and it begins nibbling on a weed, unaware
that any day has ever been anything
but this day, this shade, this impossibly soft, cool dirt.

From the porch, the hospital rises in the path
of the ladled moon, all that's left of the night sky
besides the reflection produced by the waste
of energy production. The hospital drones
into the haze that is our sky, made of everything
that exists in a hospital: heart attacks, strokes,
gonorrhea—also births, miracle births, births that defy
nature, that require the diamonds to hover.

The moon above the hospital, the night cooling—
then one of the couple, who we sometimes glimpse
doing normal things in the window facing us,
in the house between me and that droning hospital,
that monstrosity of even corners—she flashes
across the window, is gone within and I wonder
why the moon wouldn't feel the same way.

Visiting Detroit, I turn down a ride from the station
and take the Grand River bus back to Rosedale.
It's packed on a warm summer afternoon. A drunk
stumbles around the small clearing in the aisle
near the back doors. The other riders let him be.
He gets out on a block empty but for a liquor store.
I see a red-winged blackbird emerge from the cattails
of a swampy empty lot. The trees south of Warren Avenue
are lush and full, maybe wild enough to talk together.

I walk Brétton Drive from Grand River toward home.
In the park, kids play baseball. Same league as me,
under the same oak tree behind the same backstop.
I stop with my bags to watch. The score, I learn, is close.

A grade-school classmate is there, father to a player now.
We talk. A nice, smiling guy—outwardly friendly.
Does his kid know things can be different than they are?

The oak tree's roots spread under the diamond
and the seating area. It's been holding us up all along.
Through the fights, through the marriages celebrated
at the Community House at the end of right field,
through all that these kids don't know the real meaning of.

I hit the Community House once with a line drive.
My friend pitched. Our parents watched from below
the oak tree. They laughed at our childish shit-talking.
We were losing big, but still I nailed that fastball

with an inside-out swing. It rolled between the cedars
lining the building's brick patio. I walked into third base.

It can be easy to love with simplicity as a child.
I loved this city. Trappers Alley and Michigan Avenue
were big enough. Do these children know
that the focus their faces wear betrays they too
love this city, or at least for this moment, at least—
but maybe also these are the happiest kids ever.
They are in America, playing baseball in the sun.

On Zug Island's southern edge, lake sturgeon
have returned. An isolated pair nest
where the Rouge River empties muddily
into the blue Detroit. Before white men named
the river, its mouth was a breeding ground
for this ancient armored fish. Heron, trout,
muskrats, red fox, beaver thrived. Mineral
rich, a sulfur spring-fed, the mouth resplendent.
Burial grounds dotted the landscape north of the Rouge
and the river was a sacred life. White settlers
deemed the marsh "uninhabitable," and better drained.

Samuel Zug bought the river mouth in 1836. A founder
of the Republicans, a new abolitionist party, he owned land
in Ontario set aside for runaway slaves—rumour is he ferried
them through the shrouded marsh to safety.

The Zugs found the marsh not suitable for an estate.
Had a canal, called Mud Run, dug. Didn't kill the marsh.
Their heirs sold it and other men finished the job. Reclaimed
from its natural state, the land was made a dump.
Later, an iron works, then a steel foundry.
Thousands worked on Zug Island. It still makes coke
today. The old mouth, soot against the rivers'
blue and brown, breathes over Del Ray, sends a hum
over the river to Windsor. A cry more felt than heard.

Sturgeon were considered a nuisance fish. They tore
trawling nets. Men laid their bodies out on the docks
by the hundreds and burned them—not for meat or roe,
but to be rid of them. When their dried-out bodies
were found suitable to fuel steam ships,
they were hunted to extinction's brink.

Sturgeon populations are one percent of what they were.
The old-growth forests of North America are one percent
of what they were. The shorelines are bare and human.
Attempts to rebuild sturgeon populations are ongoing.
They grow slowly, breed infrequently. They remain
    a remnant
of their past. We likely cannot undo what we've done.

Native woodpeckers learn to eat the emerald ash borer. Quagga mussels are a welcome new food for lake sturgeon. The starlings that mob the pear tree are doing what they do. The round goby from Europe feeds the cormorants returning to Lake Ontario. Thirty thousand nest on the Leslie Street Spit. Humans culled their colonies because fisherman feared cormorant overfishing. DDT cleared the birds from the lake, while overfishing continued. The walleye move north in warming water. Cormorants appear in the canal in Ottawa. Starlings and crows can be shot on sight in Ontario. Fisherman want cormorants added to that list. In an empty field in Detroit, I once saw a starling murmuration, huge like you see in their native England. Is nothing natural? Everything is? Steel, a kind of rock? Invasive movement is movement. There's a still point in transit. The lamprey suck the life from trout. They are doing what lamprey do, living. Round gobies have crossed into the Mississippi River at Chicago, where the river was reversed to ship the city's shit away from the lake. Invasive carp have stayed back from the electrified barriers to Lake Michigan because there's so much shit in the water there. They may enter instead at Lake Erie. Grass, black, silver, and bighead carp, the "Asian carp," are forgiven. They do what they do. They did not ask to be farmed, or to eat the blooms accumulated in lakes near farms. They wanted to live. Quagga mussels overtake the zebra mussels and the shit they eat is the shit gobies eat, and cormorants eat the shit-filled gobies. Sometimes I'm ashamed to be human. The cisco are not a "sexy" fish. They will not attract large crowds to the aquarium in Chicago, like the sharks do.

Cisco may be bouncing back, though, in Grand Traverse Bay. According to the Dossin Great Lakes Museum on Belle Isle, Great Lakes history begins with the brave French colonists who tamed a wild, uninhabited land. In the museum's upper decks, people gawk at shipwrecks, shipping routes, model ships. Beaver pelts are displayed, but no mention of the beaver's eradication. No mention of the beaver's name in the language of the people who first named it, of what remains of them today. Humans who like to bow hunt leaping Asian carp in rivers want to plant them in Lake Michigan. In the river, they jump because they have nowhere to go. Not so in the open lake. I'm ashamed. Due to efforts by the humans who own the rivers, salmon are slowly returning to some streams off Lake Ontario. Grass carp have been found in some streams off Lake Ontario. The blue catfish of the Illinois River can eat an adult silver carp that's twenty inches long. A native weevil can decimate an invasion of Eurasian watermilfoil. We can re-reverse the Chicago River to keep the invasives of the Mississippi away from the invasives of the lakes. We can correct our engineering with more engineering, this time from the best part of us, we swear.

The rain in Moss Park at night over the empty ball field,
a constant mist reflected in the bright stadium lights.

The elm tree sends seeds in late spring down the block
to our back porch—gifts for an impossible forest.

Drinking a Stroh's and basking in the late-afternoon sun
after swimming in the icy waters of Little Traverse Bay.

Each Joshua tree is
an undiscovered constellation
waiting to be named.

Such mortal constellations
should be named
by what the trees mean

as named by themselves—
for trees by trees,
the real folk constellations.

for Catriona

There was never any Peace North Americana.
There is only the peace that can come unto me.
The only possible still point is a within reliant
on all that is without. That is, reliant on you.

The day before our wedding was shit weather.
Like God was yelling at us with these winds.
Suit and dress bags snapped like sails.
The heaviest of the hailstorm picked up
as we walked, leaning, to the rehearsal dinner.

The next day, a calm and cloudless April afternoon,
ever of the spring, we walked out into the ebb together.

As we entered the after-party, they played the song
for our first dance. The floor cleared for us,
but we waved everyone in to join us, for if we were
really islands in the stream, then we needed
to be surrounded by our life-giving stream—you.

Two of our balloons were still in the trees out front
two weeks later, just as the buds were set to open.

American white pelicans sunning on a rare sand bar
on the tip of an island in the mangrove forest
of Florida's Ten Thousand Islands. The tide sighs.
They've rebounded well from their low point fifty years back.
The boat nears. Ducks and brown pelicans are revealed
parked on the sand between the huge white birds.

Only the raccoon among mammals is found on these islands.
It's for the birds, for the fish. The islands are connected
by the sea and each trunk and branch on an island
    is connected.
Together with itself, the root system keeps the land together.

The Pacific explodes onto a rocky outcrop just before
we enter the calm waters of the Broken Group Islands.
The fast tide sinks toward its afternoon low point.

Steller's sea lions rest on the high, dry rocks, their heads
raised to the sun as they work out their family disputes.
Nervous otters on the lower rocks, ready to swim away.
Cormorants, collected, rest wherever the mammals aren't.

Once on Blue Mountain, with blue Georgian Bay in view,
on a warm May afternoon in the sun, a great shadow
passed over me.

I thought it was a hang-glider—massive wings, black-tipped—
you could hear the wings beat, a real low, felt noise.
American White Pelican, up from Florida on your way
to the breeding grounds above Superior, Hello. Thank you
for having us.

ACKNOWLEDGEMENTS

Thank you to Invisible Publishing for taking this on, and for all the amazing work they do, and to Jeff Latosik for helping me see it through its final transformation. Thank you to Desert Pets Press and *Arc Magazine* for publishing some early versions of these poems, and to *The Puritan* for gathering together such a wonderful community.

This is a book of what I've lived, so thank you first of all to my parents. Mom, you taught me to write, and so much else. What a mess I'd be without that. Dad, you kept me honest. Warren and Jenny, you looked out for my folks and have been nothing but kind and generous. To my brothers and sisters, you were my models and caretakers. To Rosedale Park, Detroit Open School, Jack Adams Arena. To the Deweys, the Websters, all the families of Rosedale Park, with a door always open to me. To U of D Jesuit, you made me think. To all of Detroit and Michigan, you're all over the pages of this book.

To New Orleans, you're all over the pages of this book. To the people I met there, to the Original Lush Krewe, you know who you are. To Loyola New Orleans, you let me think. To

Toronto, where I wrote all this. Thank you for having me. To the University of Toronto, and especially to all the people there, to my wonderful colleagues and students. I've spent so much of the last decade there, and for that I'm grateful. To the friends, colleagues, editors, poets, writers, singers, musicians, and to everyone else who had a part in this book. To my workshopers, designers, readers, teachers, and collaborators—to Bardia Sinaee, Phoebe Wang, Laura Clarke, Vincent Colistro, Michelle Brown, Daniel Renton, Andy Verboom, Jess Taylor, Daniel Scott Tysdal, Matt Loney, Sarah York, Graham Arnold, Brooke Lockyer, Denielle Van Bakel, Kate Jenks, Nate Jung, Sean Ward, Michael Laughlin, Cal Freeman, Rosemary Sullivan, Jeff Parker, Dionne Brand, Andrew Dubois, Spencer Gordon, Tyler Willis, Jason Freure, André Forget, Eric Overton and Jill Butler, Scott Marrentette, and so many more.

To my lovely wife, Catriona. You are my life. Let's do this forever.

INVISIBLE PUBLISHING is a not-for-profit publishing company that produces contemporary works of fiction, creative non-fiction, and poetry. We're small in scale, but we take our work, and our mission, seriously: We publish material that's engaging, literary, current, and uniquely Canadian.

We are committed to publishing diverse voices and experiences. In acknowledging historical and systemic barriers, and the limits of our existing catalogue, we strongly encourage writers of colour to submit their work.

Invisible Publishing is also home to the Bibliophonic, Snare, and Throwback series.

If you'd like to know more please get in touch:
info@invisiblepublishing.com

Invisible Publishing
Halifax & Picton